Sarah Kitty's
RESCUE
ADVENTURE

Written by
Michael Schor

Illustrated by
Iva Dukić

Sarah Kitty's Rescue Adventure

Paperback ISBN 978-1-960007-23-0
eBOOK ISBN 978-1-960007-24-7

Published by
Little Blessing Books
an imprint of
Orison Publishers, Inc.
PO Box 188, Grantham, PA 17027
www.OrisonPublishers.com

Dedication

This book is dedicated to brave Sarah who brightened
so many lives in such a short time.

In a small and quiet house,
In a small and quiet town,
There lived a mean old woman,
Who threw her old cat out.
There really was no reason,
For this cruel and senseless act.
The woman was simply tired
Of caring for this poor cat.

1

The cat was old and feeble.
And feeling scared and down.
She didn't deserve
to spend her days,
In a strange
and unknown town.

The weather was warm and pleasant.
Spring had just begun.
But this old, abandoned kitty
Was always on the run.

As days turned into weeks,
The cat was losing hope
That she'd ever find relief
From trying to hide and cope.

Now spring has turned to summer,
In this small and quiet town.
The day is now so steaming hot,
That not a soul's around.

The cat is getting weaker.
She needs a safe, new home.
She cries out for her mean old mom,
But alas she is alone.

Her once-new, shiny collar,
with the pretty silver bells,
Is now all black and rusty.
It itches and it smells.

She finds a shady willow,
A refuge from the sun.
She is so sick and tired
Of living on the run.

A friendly soul spies kitty.
He leaves a plate of food.
She quickly runs to eat it,
But she cannot even chew.
Her gums are red and swollen.
She lives her life in pain.
She needs a kitty doctor,
To help her eat again.

The man sees she's in trouble.
He sees that she's alone.
He wants to help poor kitty
find a safe and happy home.

He snaps a kitty photo
And posts it on Facebook.
"Kitty needs your help," he writes.
"Please do more than look."

Just across this tiny town,
This sorry post is seen.
A man who's eating breakfast
Drops his spoon and screams.
"Someone needs to save this cat.
She's thin and must have fleas.
But that 'someone' may never come,
So that someone must be me!"

The townsfolk call him Catman.
He rescues homeless cats.
They're in all shapes and sizes—
Some skinny and some fat.

He rushes out to find her
With a cat trap and some food.
He hopes to save this kitty
And brighten up her mood.

Kitty sees him coming
And ducks behind a tree.
She senses that he loves her
And doesn't try to flee.
He lays the trap beside her,
With yummy treats inside.
It's covered with a towel,
So she can go inside and hide.

Kitty smells the luscious treats…
And walks into the trap.
"Bang!" The door, it closes.
Catman starts to clap.

She thought her life was over,
But it's only just begun.
The poor, sick cat is finally safe
And doesn't have to run.

He rushes to the kitty,
Who is crying in the cage.
He's never seen a feline
So advanced in age.
She's skinny and she's balding.
But to him, she is a treasure.
The love he feels for this old cat
Is beyond all weight and measure.

"Beauty dwells within," he says,
As he takes her to his car.
He drives to the cat doctor.
It isn't very far.

"I will call you Sarah,"
Says Catman to the cat.
"Sarah means 'wise princess.'
And that will settle that."

The kindly vet sees Catman
And greets him with a hug.
"Helping strays is just my job."
He smiles and he shrugs.

The vet examines Sarah.
Catman sits and prays.
The news he gets is very sad.
Sarah's sick with AIDS.

Catman takes old Sarah,
To his rescue-kitty home—
A little house called "Catville,"
Where she will never be alone.

CATVILLE

The house does not look special.
It's kind of small and drab.
But to the residents of Catville,
It's nothing less than fab.

Some cats there started homeless
And slept out on the ground.
Some, like Sarah, lost their homes,
But now are safe and sound.

The cats see Catman coming,
With Sarah in a crate.
They run to meet and greet her.
They meow to celebrate.

26

Cat AIDS is contagious
When kitties scratch and bite.
So Sarah has her own new room
And will not get into fights.

The other cats rejoice—
They have a wise new friend!
And Sarah has a home at last,
A place to heal and mend.

28

www.ingramcontent.com/pod-product-compliance
Lightning Source LLC
Chambersburg PA
CBHW041604120626
46551CB00002B/309